The Intuitive Messages Handbook

Marisa Maney B.A., M.S.Ed.

BALBOA.PRESS

A DIVISION OF HAY HOUSE

Balboa Press books may be ordered through booksellers or by contacting:

Balboa Press
A Division of Hay House
1663 Liberty Drive
Bloomington, IN 47403
www.balboapress.com
844-682-1282

Print information available on the last page.

ISBN: 978-1-9822-5508-4 (sc)
ISBN: 978-1-9822-5509-1 (e)

Balboa Press rev. date: 09/24/2020

Dedication

To my family who I love and appreciate more than words could express.

My parents who have been by my side and have shown me unconditional love since the day I was born.

To my husband, a true gift. You have accepted me as I am from the day we met. Our relationship is a true blessing. Thank you for being the father of the most precious daughter one could hope for.

To Kazmira, you are my inspiration. You are the person in my life I value to the moon and stars and back again.

Without all of you my life would be incomplete. Love you all always and forever.

Contents

Foreword

I was at a time in my life where despite hitting professional highs and checking the boxes of achievement on the way, I was despondent and unfulfilled. A friend had mentioned seeing Marisa in passing and I reached out to her on a whim. I thought that talking with her would, at the very least, provide some insight. That her gift of intuition provide me with answers, but I did not expect that her background in counseling would show me that I already had them.

Marisa challenged me to think deeper. To delve beyond the superficial road map of what society deems success. To examine my emotions and reactions with an honesty I didn't even realize I had the capacity for. She compelled me, someone prone to quick and thoughtless reactions, to stop and sincerely contemplate my answers. To respond authentically without sarcasm or guile. Our interactions brought to light so many seemingly insignificant events, that upon deeper reflection, came to the surface to be recognized and processed.

In the years that I have worked with Marisa, I have grown in unimaginable ways. We still maintain our bi-monthly sessions, addressing things that come up and she continues to push me to dig deeper. She has provided me the tools to stop focusing on my perceived shortcomings and to celebrate who I am. Through her patience and tutelage, I am no longer pursuing a set of standards incongruent with my life's genuine purpose. I now appreciate and honor the emotions I am feeling, for a fuller understanding and acceptance of myself.

Marisa has been an extraordinary guide on my journey of self-discovery. This book and its questions encompass the ethos of her practice. It is an extension of her, an inspiring introspective exploration towards self-love and fulfillment.

Preface

Everyone could tap into messages from the universe, a higher power or whatever source they feel brings them universal connection and knowledge. The only limitations are earthly fears, frustrations, and the lack of confidence. This book has been almost ten years in the making with another twelve years of experience behind it. It is a collection of messages that have been given to me to pass on to others with the purpose of helping people to walk the path that has been laid out in front of them with grace and strength.

Coming to a point in my life where I became riddled with anxiety and panic attacks with no apparent source, I sought many holistic methods to help ease my distress. Throughout the journey I discovered hypnosis: The power of allowing someone to help you to access the solitude that lies within. An unintended result of my sessions was the opening of the door to my untapped intuitive potential. Being able to intensely relax the mind offered a path for me to feel energy I would otherwise not notice.

Many people do not believe that it is possible to reach beyond what we can see and hear to have a deeper understanding of the energy around us. I began to receive messages in the form of thoughts that I was guided to give to others. I was unsure of where they were coming from. I was compelled to share information with people about their energy, their lives and even give them signs and symbols from loved ones who have passed. Although at the time it was stressful and I often thought I was "losing my mind", I have accepted this gift. Thankfully, I am of sound mind, despite what some people may think, until they talk with me and they are able to see what I do.

Keeping my intentions positive and focused on helping others, I have brought many people great relief with my messages. I do not prefer to be called a psychic even though most people do identify my gifts in that way. I look at myself as an intuitive person who has a mission to help others to see who they are from another perspective, a view not of another person but of the reflection of their energy. When I work with people, I share what lies ahead, sometimes behind that got them to their current place in life. My goal is always to support others to open their hearts to their own intuition and to offer them a view of what vast unique ability each human has in this world but most importantly how vital it is that people love, appreciate, and trust themselves.

An important part of my life's work is to help people along their journey to be happy and healthy. Once people move away from their apprehension toward life and their lack of confidence in themselves and their path in life, they can move mountains. I thoroughly hope you enjoy these messages and find peace within the words on the pages as well as the joy of freedom you receive from being awakened to your power and importance in this world.

Acknowledgment

I want to thank everyone who has been on my life's journey and has given me the opportunity to grow and use my skills for the betterment of myself and others.

James Lee, your ability to use hypnosis and vast healing capabilities gave me the strength to accept my gifts and grow into all that I am today.

Dr. Amanda Fey, a true gift in my life. Naturopathic medicine is a modality that everyone should be blessed to access. You have walked me through the toughest times and continue to be my trusted source for the health of my body and mind. You always work with others under the rule of patience and love.

Melissa Ouimette, you taught me about the necessity to relax the body and mind. Your skills working with energy healing are amazing.

Finally, to all of my clients who trust and appreciate me, I am pleased to put this handbook out for you. As always, I wish you peace, happiness, and an appreciation for your life.

Introduction

When I work with others, I feel that trust is of utmost importance. There is a level of vulnerability when someone decides to meet with another person to learn more about healthy living, managing emotions, and big life choices. My journey has given me the tools to understand others and to have a sense of empathy. It was important to me that I attain a level of education that would enrich my life and allow me to offer something of value to this world. Studying sociology and earning a master's degree in education with an emphasis on counseling has given me the knowledge needed to understand people and how they interact in their personal lives and within society. My life experiences have afforded me the emotional intelligence to understand, relate to, and connect with others.

I have a distinct understanding of what the struggle with anxiety feels like. Life experiences are our best teacher. Aside from acute issues, working with hundreds of people of all ages over the past twenty years, has given me a beautiful palette of experiences to pull from. I use the additional unique level of intuitiveness that has come into my life which enables me to help others to grow hope and healthy outlooks. People have used my messages combined with their own instincts to bring out their truth. Everyone has the answers within to life's biggest queries. With some guidance and prompting, wonderful growth happens.

The messages in this book are a combination of my education, experiences as well as missives that come to me from a source that I cannot define. You may call it deep intuition, a gift from beyond, or the source. I write the words that come through my hands, when I read them back, I feel inspired and enlightened. I know that anyone reading the narration needs the energy being relayed and will benefit from it. Many of these statements though this book have questions for you to answer, there is work to be done. Messages alone cannot resolve all your challenges.

Being honest with yourself and feeling the emotions that arise when you explore these ideas will open your best course for personal tranquility. Each chapter will start with a story that is a combination of experiences people have had related to the topic. These stories will give you a minute to walk in someone else's shoes. A chance to possibly relate to the fact that many life experiences are shared.

The way that you access this book is completely up to you, but my idea behind its use is that you open the book when you feel you need some inspiration or guidance. Open to any page, that page or paragraph you see will be your message for the day or moment. The words will be aligned with what you are seeking. Of course, feel free to read through the book or look to a specific chapter for guidance. The messages you find will be energetically aligned to your needs. Many of the lessons may seem similar but worded in a unique way. This is important because messages will resonate in various ways at different times for the reader. There are very simple ways to improve your life, outlook, and experiences. It may take time to understand the messages and work with them but when you learn how to view your encounters from a place of growth, a whole new world will open to you.

I wish you peace, love, confidence, contentment, and the power to realize you have all you need within to lead your best life.

Self-Love

Loving and valuing yourself is the first key to success in every aspect of your life. Self-love does not mean you are selfish; it is not a negative trait. It is imperative that you value and love yourself inside and out. When you feel compassion and care for yourself you will be able to live a full life and give your best to others.

A Story on Self-Love

There are so many things that happen in a lifetime that chip away at one's self-esteem. Things that we choose or that happen to us. Not to mention how people come into this world. Your personality combined with life experiences will dictate how you deal with self-love.

Her first words to me when she sat down were, "I hate myself". Usually it takes people some time to get to that statement. They will use softer ways to let me know that they are struggling. When I asked, "What do you hate about yourself?" I got a list. A long one. "I don't like how I look, how I respond to others, how I allow the world to treat me. I hate that I am sensitive, I want to be young again. I don't like anything about myself". I asked that she explore each of these topics with me and we had a conversation about self-love pertaining to each theme in her life that she had concerns about.

Her assignment was to take each of these beliefs and challenge them as they came in. Day by day, moment by moment. Treating herself as her own best friend. I asked her the question, "Would you agree with a best friend or someone you love if they were to make these types of statements out loud in front of you"? She quickly responded, "No, I would look for their best traits to reinforce their self-worth". When I asked why she will not afford that same support to herself she started to have an awakening.

We worked on ideas that would help her to understand her role in healing herself. I continued with questions over the weeks and months for her to explore. What would it feel like to look in a mirror and accept, appreciate, and love what you see? How would your responses to others be in your life if you had confidence and your feelings about yourself did not hinge on the acceptance of others? Would you allow people to treat you with disrespect or control you if you valued your own opinions? How could you look at your sensitivity as a gift not a curse? Aging, what are you missing or fearing when you think about aging? This is a lot of emotion to process at once so breaking each feeling up over time offered the resolve needed.

When she realized she could challenge her own thoughts, her life changed in drastic ways for the good.

She reported using the replacement thoughts about herself, her achievements, and her goals. Learning to love herself was the key that opened many doors. She started used her newfound confidence to set boundaries in her relationship. She gained the courage to stand up for her ideas and wishes in life. She reported that her work life had improved because she looked for and found value in her duties and abilities. She had experienced so much personal growth that when I saw her years later it was like meeting a whole new person. She was ready to let go of her limited thinking and move into her life. It was a beautiful transformation. It all started with her being ready to make changes and her victory came from slow and steady work.

Messages about Self-love

Stop hating yourself for all that you are not; love yourself for all that you are.

The first person you should be thinking of is yourself. Many people struggle with liking themselves for multiple reasons. Everyone's behaviors are driven by what they think of themselves and how they perceive the world. Working on valuing your external and internal self will be the answer to every one of your questions in life. Try it: think of a challenge you face. If you valued yourself and had a strong sense of self love, how would your experiences be different?

_____

_____

_____

Take care of you.

It is okay to take a pause, do what you want, and look out for yourself.

It is time to start giving yourself a break and permission to accept how you feel at any given moment and do what you want to do. Being the mentally healthiest that you can be takes planning. The result of working on keeping yourself in a positive mental state is a stable life for you and everyone in your life. Constructive mental health comes from the ability to know your limits. The happier you are, the more contented people around you will be. Take a break; take care of yourself.

One true love.

The one and only thing to master in your life is to love, value, and appreciate yourself. With this confidence, you will never allow yourself or anyone else or thing to hurt you. You will not accept being slighted, mistreated, or taken advantage of. You will not hurt yourself with poor decision making. Achieving self-love will heal every area of your life. Think about your career, love life, friendships, parenting, and personal health. If you were your first love how would your life look? Ask yourself this question every time a challenge arises: If I truly loved and appreciated myself and my choices would I be facing this issue the same way? You will always get the same answer.

_____

_____

_____

Stay or go?

Love is not all you need. You need the real components of love like respect, honesty, trust, a soft place to land, reassurance, loyalty, and true happiness. People need these experiences both from themselves and others. You matter. How you are treated matters. Self-esteem means everything. Without it, people burn up precious minutes of their lives surrounding themselves with internal pain, unworthy people, and negative situations. The easy path only looks easy; it rarely is.

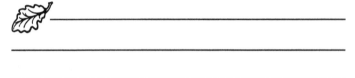

May your inner voice be the kindest you know.

It is crucial that people find their best friend within themselves.

If you do not have compassion, kindness, empathy, and appreciation for yourself you cannot have it fully for anyone else. The lack of a positive relationship with the self may lead to dysfunctional relationships, poor mental and physical health, and overall dissatisfaction. People try at times to dispute this but after true exploration they always come back to it seeing the truth. Self-appreciation leads to the ability to set healthy boundaries, make positive decisions, and live life to the fullest.

What if you devoted yourself to you?

Devotion to yourself means that you take your opinions, emotions, and feelings into account fully. You would have stronger relationships, be a better parent, be happier at work, be physically healthier, be less anxious/

depressed/angry. You would have more tolerance, more stamina, and more joy.

_____

_____

_____

Authenticity.

Do you consider yourself to be an authentic person? One of the most complicated tasks in life is to analyze yourself. It is difficult to make healthy connections with others when you do not trust or even know the true you. Being vulnerable with yourself and others will allow you to experience feelings and emotions. Do you bury your emotions? Do you hide from yourself and others emotionally? Do you own your feelings?

_____

_____

_____

Transparency.

Transparency is being real. Being true to what you want in life. Being faithful to others. Being open and honest about your experiences and values. Do you accept your decisions? Do you lie to yourself and others? Do you hurt other people because of your pain? Do you own your behaviors? What would your life look like by exploring these attributes? What would it feel like to wake up every day knowing you are living authentically? You can restart your life in any moment. Be the leader in your life; no one else is going to do it for you.

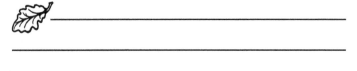

You and your tribe.

People who love and respect themselves inherently have a tribe of loving people surrounding them. That is a natural consequence of confidence.

The sooner you work on self-appreciation, respect, and love, the sooner you will be living in that world. It is time to step up your game. Life is moving through you and you do not have unlimited time. Make yourself your best friend and watch the positive people that start to surround you. In the end, you only have yourself to gain strength from. No one can save you from yourself; you have all the power you need.

Self-observation.

What if you looked at challenges, heartache, and pain as this; opportunity for happiness? How many experiences can you think of in your life that you have survived through that were horribly hurtful, but you used these encounters to build strength? A shattered heart, broken body, tired soul: all signs and opportunities to learn more about yourself and the world around you. Experiences are put on your path for you to learn how to engage with yourself and others in a healthy way. When you bottle up emotions, use shame, blame, or guilt against yourself or you hurt others in response to your pain, this is where you will get stuck. Stepping back and watching your life, taking a true inventory of where you have been, how you have reacted and what you can change through slow and concentrated efforts will lead you to peace.

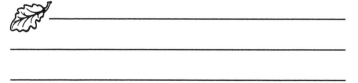

Ask for help.

There is no shame in getting help from someone to make your life a better place to be. The negative stigma of seeking professional assistance is thankfully becoming less prevalent but it is still out there in some people's eyes. Remember that others have not walked in your shoes. Their opinion of you is none of your business; your life is none of theirs. Having someone there to help you to find your truth is the best gift you can give yourself. Think of all the bandages you try and use in your life to make frustration, pain, and confusion be hidden. By using substances or food or any distracting behavior, people try to bury their pain. Reaching out to have help will not take up your time or money- it will give you a life worth living. Find your helper and love your life.

Self-limitation.

A great practice for all humans is to challenge the negative, self-limiting talk that comes through the mind. People have a strong knack for being critical of themselves, their actions, and their thoughts. What can you do to change this behavior?

An amazing aspect of our brains is that habits and thinking patterns can be changed. Every time a negative thought comes in you may choose to challenge it with a positive thought or attribute about yourself or your life. Taking the power away from the limited habitual response of your brain will give you the stamina to live without limits. The longer you practice this, the changes in your brain will take hold. You can always find something good within or around you.

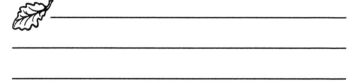

Power.

We all have the right and ability to take our power back at any time. Take it back from society, other individuals or our own selves. No one is unequal to another. We all deserve respect, acceptance, and love. Our worth should not hinge on what others provide for us or do for us but what we do for ourselves both internally and externally. It is time to shift the energy of oppression and reliance to a strong self-advocating energy. Self-love leads to command of respect. It leads to the ability to stand up for yourself. It leads to you living a full life.

Who you are now?

You only have who you are, in the life you are in, right at this moment.

You are not the you from any number of years ago. Your life is not what it was. It is what it is now. It does not matter what happened in the past or what is happening tomorrow. Often people have a vision of what their life "should" be. Who they "should" be. What good does that do for anyone? You always have a choice, even if it is difficult, to live in this very moment and accept what is. You certainly can set intentions to change how you see the world, or change a situation you are in. To grow and move you must start where you are in the moment. Work on fully accepting yourself and your life. Understand that your choices got you where you are. Know that your decisions will take you where you are going. Want to change? Start from a good spot. Right here, right now.

The root of you.

As each day passes, your life shifts around you and you must change to accommodate it. Your soul is always working to serve your highest good. This means that there is always a healthy path in front of you. There is a root within you that knows who you are as a person. Despite what has happened to you since the day you were born, your soul has a fundamental belief in your role on this planet. Look within and explore your place in this world and your duty to yourself and others. Remember who you are, strip away all that you have experienced, and be true to your soul. If you struggle with anything: investigate the challenge, remember your convictions, go back to your root self.

Influences.

If someone or something is influencing you and it does not feel right, that is your intuition attempting to warn you to slow down and make a choice.

The most important person in your life is you. Start holding your spirit and who you are to the highest standards. If you love, trust, and value who you are then nothing can harm you. You will make only the best choices and put yourself in situations that serve your callings and highest good. Think of the people you love: What do you do for them? What guidance do you offer them? Why aren't you doing those things for yourself?

New day new you.

What are you going through? What lesson are you learning? The happiest and most difficult times of life are not good or bad luck. Everything is put on your path to help you grown to your highest ability. Look at your life right now. What emotions are attached to the events happening around you? What patterns do you long to release? What are you hoping to embrace? Everything that "happens" leads you down a road to explore. Every day you have a new opportunity to be the best version of yourself. You know what to do to make your life comfortable, peaceful, and joyous. Listen to your mind, body, and soul.

_____

_____

_____

Pay attention.

Your physical body will always reflect your emotional state. It reveals how much you value yourself. Physical ailments are often rooted in emotion. There is no pain, disease or physical experience that does not have an emotional component. The key to healing yourself is acceptance, release of emotion, and thoroughly embracing each moment of your life. Life is both simple and worthy of difficult personal exploration at the same time. Never lose an opportunity to learn the lesson behind the experience. Listen to your body and find the connection to your mind.

Welcome all that comes into your life, into your life; love it for all that it is.

You know what is best.

Often you will not trust your intuition. You may scramble within your own mind to manage your days. We could all hear the messages that surround us if we trust ourselves. Work on hearing your intuition, you will learn the difference between what calls out to you from deep within compared to the crazy chatter of your mind. Step one is being honest with yourself. Stopping the cycle of protecting your emotions will help you awaken to your intuition. Feeling the grief, shame, joy, and bliss we all carry equally will help you to value instincts.

Acceptance.

Accept yourself on every level. Meet yourself where you are. It is fine to be in a place of uncertainty or on the contrary in a place of great comfort. Accept it all. Feel that deep sense of "knowing" and move toward it. Loving, trusting, and believing in yourself and your path takes time but step by step, day by day, and situation by situation, it can be done. Move into your day with faith in yourself.

Trust

**Trusting in the process of life, believing
in yourself, having faith in others.**

A Story about Trust...

There are various types of trust that people experience:
Trust in one's self. Trust in the universe. Trust in the path
of life. Trust in others.

She was having a difficult time living in the moment.
Trusting a journey that she had co-created with the
universe. It is a tricky concept to release the memories
of the past and the stresses about the future. The need to
control what is happening is strong for most people.

She had a tumultuous childhood. Parents who had
multiple challenges. She was responsible to keep the family
safe from each other. There was violence, a lack of trust,
and instability. As she grew older, she carried her instincts
to protect herself and others. She did not willingly trust
people. This caused great rifts in her relationships. She
would unknowingly sabotage her connections with
others. Always feeling hurt and alone.

We worked on taking each day and focusing on what was happening in the moment. Trusting how she felt. Understanding emotions and sentiments from others. We did some exercises about walking in the shoes of those around her. We explored the fact that others will not always understand her perspective.

Her responsibility was first to trust herself. Allowing feelings to roll in and out like the waves of the ocean helped her to visualize the pain and hurt moving through her. The more tolerant she became, trusting what was happening around and within her, the stronger she became.

She began to work on relationship expectations and goals. Accepting that it was safe to trust life led her on a path of success both internally and within relationships.

I had the pleasure of being in a social situation with her and her family about a year into us working together. The greatest joy was seeing her with her children, trusting her instincts, believing in them to make good decisions, believing the moment she was in was just what it was meant to be.

Messages about Trust

Confidence.

Look within your mind for your answers but do not question too much. There is a time to question but there is also a time to trust thoughts that come by learning to distinguish between emotional/ behavioral ideas and divine direction. When thoughts are obsessive or driven by an emotion, they are most often created by the mind. They mean nothing. Divine thoughts come in gently like whispers and your soul identifies with them. They are comfortable. They will not cause fear, even if they do not seem the most positive. Listen to your heart for intervention, not your mind. Trust your soul, it knows what you need. Have confidence in the energy surrounding you.

Your eyes can close; your heart always stays open.

What happens when we do not allow ourselves to feel emotions, gut instincts, or the cries of our soul to pay attention? We get ill. Physically and emotionally.

You cannot trick yourself into believing negative experiences or life choices are okay. Your spirit will always work toward your truth. Walk away from anything that is not serving your highest good. The journey of change may be tough, but the reward will be much better than the voyage to nowhere. Walking away does not always mean physically. Life situations sometimes leave us having to deal with tough people and physical living situations.

You absolutely can emotionally shift to help and protect yourself at any time, even if you cannot physically change your situation in the moment. You always have the choice as to how to respond to a situation.

You have the answers.

Today is a day to start to trust yourself and your intuition. People get caught up in their minds and the rules of society. The expectations of who and what we should be and how we must live our lives forces us to put our instincts aside. When you abandon a path that you know is right for you to appease others, you are just creating a tougher journey for yourself. You always know what to do. The only problems are the noise of your mind and the external world. In the end, all that matters is that you live a life true to your calling. Be with those you love, do what you adore, and strive to appreciate your life. Put the "shoulds" and "coulds" aside. Go out there and live your own life fearlessly.

Trust your path.

Trust that you are where you are meant to be. Remember there are infinite possibilities in life. Acknowledge your gifts and love life to the fullest. Most importantly, be content with who you are. You are perfect and have a distinct purpose in life. Many people treat themselves terribly. Choosing yourself to be your own best friend will lead you to see how easily you are able to change your world. Trusting in yourself and what resonates with you every day will allow you to walk your best journey.

Nothing is wrong.

It is important to remember that everything that has happened, positive or negative is for your highest good and experiences are stepping stones on your path in life.

All is well, you are okay, you will be okay. We are all experiencing grief from the loss of our past. People, experiences, even the ways we all change over time may leave a space within. How to move forward? Step into the moment of what is now. Trust that you are where you are supposed to be and feeling how you are intended to be feeling at this very moment. Why? You will know why as time moves on. The lessons, the growth, the experiences are what make you who you are. Challenge yourself to accept what is, feel your way through each moment, and know all is well.

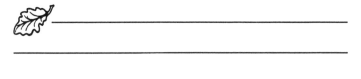

Exquisite life.

As the saying goes, the grass is green where you water it. You are exactly where you should be at this exact moment. Trust the universe for putting you where you are right now. Every part of your life is divinely ordered for your highest good. So, settle into the moments as they come. Embrace the happy times, and accept the challenges with a "thank you for a lesson". Take a breath, water your grass, and stay on your side of the fence where your life is just fine.

Your purpose.

You have a purpose, you are important, you can choose to grip onto fear (grief, sadness, depression, anxiety) or choose to pull your blessings closer (your calling, people you love, your health; no matter the challenges, your home, your future). What is your true intent? Do you trust yourself to relax into what is meant for you?

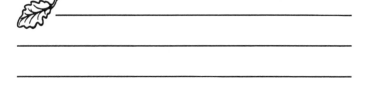

_____

_____

Universal order.

Your life is not just a series of random events. Your spirit has a clear and knowing path to follow. You are in a body to live a life, learn lessons, and reach a higher place for your soul. You are given a series of challenges to overcome. The experiences, people, and life events are all on your path for you to face, accept, and work through. No matter what your beliefs, there is an order to life that cannot be denied once you take in all that is surrounding you.

Your theme.

Everyone has a theme to his/her life. Is it dealing with low self-esteem? Fear? Guilt? Success? Anger? Shame? Intense love? Addiction (escaping life)? Peace? There is no "good" or "bad" experience. That is a human construct. Your soul only sees potential for growth in every opportunity. Today go into the world trying to understand what your spirit is asking of you. Trust and acceptance are the keys to happiness. You can only change the way you respond to a situation; you may not be able to immediately alter a situation once you bring it into your life. The only thing certain in life is change and your lack of control of what happens "to" you. When you have an emotional reaction, look beneath it to the true feelings, do not bury them, explore them. Find your theme; is it what you want it to be?

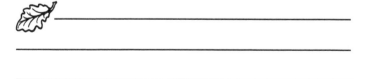

Guidance.

Humans have a unique gift to be guided by intuition. You get messages all the time to light your path. The struggle is that our conscious minds get in the way to distract the messages. If you are getting repetitive thoughts and hearing them being reinforced all around you may want to pay attention. What is trying to be relayed to you? True guidance is not scary or urgent, honest nudges feel safe and secure even if they are not positive. Look deeper and ask is it related to an emotion that you need to acknowledge? Is it something that you need to change? Is it something that you could accept more readily?

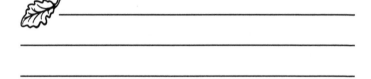

Only two ways.

There are truly only two ways to walk your live life: With fear or love. Fear will lead you to live with feelings like anxiety, depression, or avoidance behaviors (hurting yourself or others through dominance, control, substance abuse, etc.). Love will allow you to see experiences as lessons. You will embrace the moment and live there. You will have love, appreciation, and be tolerant of yourself and others. Few people live on the path of love. You can start in the very next breath. Your life is worth it.

Relationships

Our lives our built around the connections that we have with ourselves and others. The bonds that we have could be challenges or true blessings. Our feelings about ourselves and our responses to others in relationships will dictate the path the bond takes.

A Story about Relationships....

Just like all relationships in life, love relationships could push our emotions to the limits of what we feel we can withstand.

She was betrayed. The hurt was immense. The trust was gone. What ended this relationship? Was it the way he belittled her around people in their life? Was it that he did not respect her opinions? Was it that he lived his life with no thought of what she needed or wanted from a relationship? No. Even though this went on for many years.

The reason for the end was that he was spending time and developing relationships with other women. The ultimate betrayal in her eyes and to any relationship.

Could she see the signs of what was to come? Did she see any of the other early relationship violations as a breach of trust? No. People tolerate a lot from the ones they love and often wonder what they missed when things get to the point of demise. It is important to pay attention to how others treat us, and to care about how we feel when we are with the ones we love. Just because we love someone, it does not always mean we should be in a relationship with them.

The biggest issue she faced was the lack of a healthy connection with herself. She did not have the self-respect or feel he was worthy of someone who valued her completely. Her husband's affairs were the result of a deep lack of honesty, respect, and love. The results for her were more hurt and blame which she directed toward herself.

While working through the flawed expectations and views she experienced in the relationship, she learned more about what she deserved in life. She learned more about boundaries and what a valuable relationship looks like.

Exploring all aspects of partnerships in their fullest forms will help to guide you on a clearer path when building connections with yourself and others. Being in the moment of healthy relationships and not having to look back to see the flaws that led to a demise is a beautiful way to live.

Her success came when she released the relationship and did it with love. She had anger, resentment, and pain but that did not stop her from using the emotions to build a new vision and goals for what she wants in her next relationship.

She continued to work with me for many years. She found a partner who was worthy of her love, and she found a great appreciation and devotion to herself. Having children in a loving relationship has made her life complete. Being able to raise youngsters with emotional intelligence has brought her great peace. It is never too late to change the path of any relationship and lead a life of love, happiness, and satisfaction.

Messages about Relationships

Friend.

What is a friend? Are you a good one? It is time to explore friendship and grow, reflect, heal, or improve your interpersonal relationships. What is a healthy friend? Someone who is kind, nonjudgmental, caring, empathetic and loyal. Someone who you know will have your back. A person who likes you just the way you are. Someone who would never intentionally hurt you. If they do make a mistake, they own it and try to make it better. A friend is not jealous. They may envy something in your life, but they celebrate your joys with you. They mourn your sadness. They hope to lift you up, never bring you down. They will be honest with you even if it hurts a bit. Everyone needs at least one person they could call a true friend. To have a healthy friend you must be a healthy friend. Who can you trust? Who are the first people who come to mind when you think of friends? How do you show appreciation for your friends? Today, say thank you to people who matter to you.

_____

_____

_____

Take care.

What is your inner child? We are all just ourselves as children covered in a larger body. Picture your soul as an egg. The yolk is the little you, as a child with all the experiences you had wrapped by a shell, your evolving life. Which is the richest part of the egg, the part that leads to your growth? Your inner child. Spend time focusing on nurturing that part of you. Just because we grow, the happiness, sadness, fears, joys, grief, excitement, and trauma we experienced does not just go away. We need to process these emotions as adults to help make sense of them. How? Spend time being kind, loving and understanding of your inner child. Treat him/ her with respect. Do some activities to support yourself. Do something that brings you joy and peace. Play, go into the world, and be carefree. Give your soul some time off from the pressures of adult life.

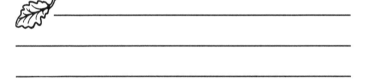

Mirror work.

When you walk by a mirror, look into your eyes, and tell yourself you are loved, beautiful, wanted, and important. That you are perfect the way you are. That you have a purpose. These are all the words you should have heard as a child. You may have heard these things often; you may have never heard them once.

We all would benefit from nurturing ourselves first and looking beyond the shell of the life around us to the gentle, innocent child inside.

Mothers.

People all did not experience the Hallmark version of a mom. Moms are flawed humans like all of us. They do the best they can with who they are. Sometimes what they have to offer is limited. A mother may have been harsh or dismissive. She may have not been physically or emotionally supportive. On the other hand, a mother may have been phenomenal. She may have been emotionally and physically healthy, well balanced, and wonderful. No matter who your mom is or was, or what type of mother you are or have chosen to be, it is time to honor the human spirit for everyone come from a mother. Honor the fact that all people face challenges and limitations but, in the end, your best is good enough. Use today for gratitude for what you have or had in your life due to your mother. Review the strengths and weaknesses you have endured. Realize the impact your experiences have had in your world and how you may use them to better your current life.

A visit.

Relationships do not end when people die. When we die what happens? Energy will leave the body and where does it go? It surrounds us all. Who is the first person that you think of when you hear "Heaven"? Loved ones send thoughts, symbols, and signs to the living. A message to let go of fear, to step up and live your life, to let love, peace, honesty, and passion lead you. You are loved, strong and you are enough. Your

family and close friends know your value both in life
and death.

_____

_____

_____

Love.

What is love? Appreciation of one's self, a feeling
of warmth toward others, a respect for all life, an
understanding that we all are one. The goosebumps,
tears, smiles, fears, laughter, love, joy, pain, and sorrow.
The fierce protection of family and deep care for friends.
Everyone is someone's family member, child, friend. We
are no different from one another in any way when it
comes to love. Challenge yourself to truly love yourself,
others, and life. Notice love all around and within
you. Recognizing love is the best way to experience it
throughout every day.

_____

_____

_____

Children.

Raising children is difficult. The goal is to bring up
a healthy, happy adult. We often will try to fix problems
rather than meet kids where they are so they may learn

how to manage their own emotions. Sometimes people react with fear when children show emotion. Adults may get angry or controlling. This is often because they have never learned how to process their own emotions.

What if adults responded with love? With empathy and active listening? People may think about avoiding threats, yelling, or controlling. Taking a moment to ask yourself how you would like someone to respond to you in times when things are rough could make all the difference. Kids are little people with the same needs that all adults have. Start early to meet them where they are, and you will see happier adults emerge.

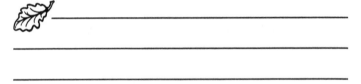

Do not crumble to keep another whole.

Staying strong and in love with ourselves requires boundaries. The people in our lives have many struggles; everyone does. To protect and allow yourself to be happy and have emotional growth in this life it is important to stay whole. Stand by your rights to be treated with respect and love. You dictate how others treat you. Remember that you allow every step of your life to happen with the choices that you make. It does not matter what hand you were dealt. There are no excuses in life. You own what you do, who you align and with, and how you react to every situation. Set yourself up for success. Love yourself unconditionally, work to your highest potential, and always be honest with yourself and others. Do not give yourself or your energy to those who are not doing all the same things. Do not settle for a partner who is not right for you because it is easy, nothing about that is easy. The choices you make will dictate everyday of your life. Always keep yourself whole.

Worthy love.

Being accepting and loving should not equal being a doormat, disrespected or abused. Who are you giving a free pass to in your life to break you down out of "love"? Be fearless when protecting your self-worth, morals, and values. You can love unconditionally but do not need to love unworthy people. You can love the memory of what you once had or once dreamt it to be if you acknowledge that is what is real. People come into our lives to teach us how to be treated.

_____

_____

Communication.

How do you interact with friends and family? We often struggle to make our view known or try to persuade others to think the way we do. This happens when we either do not have confidence or we do in fact have a passion or knowledge we want to share.

We often try to share at times when it is least effective. The only good time to open the door to discussion is when you are sure the other person is interested in communicating and examining viewpoints. If you let your ego guide you it will be very frustrating and a tremendous waste of energy. Continually giving your opinion or trying to dictate how others should feel leads to rifts in relationships. No viewpoint is "correct". People see the world through their own life lens, through their own experiences, values, and morals. You may be better off being the observer and process what others are really trying to relay. The loudest voice is often the first to be ignored. What tactics do you see people use when they are trying to get a point across? Try staying quiet and thinking about what emotion is driving what you are hearing: Anxiety, guilt, shame? Maybe an overconfidence or lack of confidence. Does the person have to be in control or present that way to maintain their own sense of self? Your response should match your goals, not someone else's.

_____

_____

_____

Soulmate.

Who teaches us the truth about love? Or any human relationship? We learn by watching family, and society, often very flawed teachers. No one explains what relationships are healthy in a true, consistent way from when we are children. We must go to school to learn how to read and write but where is real, honest, factual teaching about emotion and connections with others? We watch movies and see romantic idealized love. We hear of soulmates. We hope to all be accepted and have a wonderful full life because finally someone loves us. Shouldn't all relationships start and end with self-love? Wouldn't it be wonderful to not "need" approval or direction from anyone as a condition for love? How would it feel to fully love another with no expectations for their acceptance of us at all times?

Healthy individuals have no need to dictate anyone else's behaviors or choices. When you think if a soulmate what do you envision? How could we make the expectations about love relationships more realistic in life?

_____

_____

_____

We are all one.

Do you feel love and peace for fellow man? We are all related to one another on a soul level. With all the hatred, intolerance, negativity, division, hurt, and pain in the world, it is more important than ever to remember that we all strive for the same thing in the end. We all want to survive, love our families, protect our friends, be accepted, enjoy loved ones, be comfortable, and be at peace. Despite how people consciously or unconsciously choose to live. No matter what side or lack of side you are on, about any topic. We are all the same and have the same goals as humans. We all could love ourselves and others endlessly if we choose that. Today and moving forward, look at others as humans, not what color they are, not what they "believe" just that we are all connected. Maybe if that were everyone's focus, the energy could shift, love could prevail. Try not to allow your life experiences to pause you long enough to divide or hate. Let your human experiences guide you with humility and acceptance. Walk in love, share peace, and spread your kind soul.

 _____

_____

_____

Your Source.

Today is a day to appreciate, love, grieve, miss, yearn, strive, and hope in relationship to parents. If you are a parent, you understand the sense of loss at times as the years pass by. If you have children, it is both a joy and sadness as life moves so quickly. If you have lost your parents, there is a void that cannot be filled. Parents should be the source of your comfort in life. Comfort is what we all need as we live. Did your parents bring you comfort? Are you a comfort to your children? What can you do to help heal any negative experiences from your source? What can you do to celebrate the joy of parents no matter how large or small?

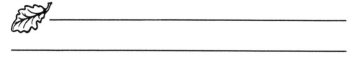

Your inner child.

Look at yourself. You are now an adult; your body has covered the little soul that still lives inside. You continue to feel every emotion that has built the adult you carry all day. Who are you at your core? How much of "you" did family and society take away or change over your lifetime? People generally do not have poor intentions raising children. They do the best they can. Sadly, it often is not in a way that allows kids to be who they are. Most children are raised to conform to an expected behavior, an anticipated outcome, a shadow of the parent or a sibling. Some people feel like robots. They are told what they like and what is good for them. Of course, children need to be raised with rules, understanding the way society works but do they really need to be told what they should value or like in life? Should you have to stretch beyond your personal limits and comfort zone just to please others? Does anyone ever need to be called lazy or stupid or told their attitude is horrible when they are not living someone else's dreams? Did anyone guide you based on who you are inside? Envision your life if you were not told who to be. What if from day one you could be just who you are. Maybe a big part of life is about undoing what has been done to you once you start exploring who you really are.

Real love.

Madly in love versus healthy, peacefully, and sanely in love. Real love is not continuous lust, longing, or constant physical interaction. It is not achieved by endless work or sacrifice of one's self. Real love is easy, kind, gentle, and secure. It is not feeling worthless or hurt by someone. It is not begging, screaming, crying, or hurting. It is trust, loyalty, and peace. Having someone physically near you to avoid being alone at any cost will actually cost you.

Step Away.

Sometimes we need to step away from people, places, or things that burn us out. Walk away from repeating family patterns or personal behaviors that do nothing positive for you. No one and nothing can hold you back as you step away and walk toward yourself.

Boundaries.

Unless someone is asking for your help or advice you would be best served by staying out of their life decisions. It will cause you and everyone else less stress.

With children your job is to give them a strong foundation. The decisions they make as they grow are theirs. With family, your place is not to control anyone. You may not agree with or like how someone else is choosing to live but just as you do not want other people's control, they do not want yours. This is a tough concept but one that people need to ponder. Live, laugh with, and love the people in your life. Move away from judging, controlling, and condemning. What would the world look like if this were practiced?

_____

_____

_____

Own it.

We are conditioned as young children to take on other people's "stuff". Sometimes we taught to clean up the emotional messes made by family members. We may be led into be unauthentic to ourselves by being forced to live the way others tell us to live. The number one need of humans is belonging. We take on everyone else's behaviors to accommodate this need. We try to morph ourselves around others so that we are not rejected. What happens?

We lose ourselves. Truly, your only responsibility is to know yourself. Think about how you were raised. What would have helped you to be mentally healthier? It is not too late to rewrite your past according to your rules and own your future.

_____

_____

_____

Complicated.

Relationships with others can be very complicated. Be it romantic, familial or friendships; we all come from a place of our own experiences and lens of life. We attempt to mesh with others often in dysfunctional ways. What if we admitted to ourselves our most vulnerable parts? Our challenges? Places we need to make some changes. What if we decided to honor ourselves with honesty, loyalty, and trust? Wouldn't it be easier to connect with others if we came from a place of authenticity? Healthy relationships are not complicated.

_____

_____

_____

Harmony.

Concerned about a relationship? Take a break from your worry. Take time to access your emotional responses when you are with others. Sometimes what you think are the worst situations end up leading you to the best outcome. Without the bad times we could never experience the good. Make sure you are honoring your soul. There is a difference between working on a mutually respectful relationship and trying to save something that should not be saved. Be honest with yourself first. Living in harmony with others comes from understanding the rhythm of life.

_____

_____

_____

Life Choices

Our choices dictate the quality of life that we have. Honor yourself with your life choices. You can always start over and have compassion for times that you do not have success from your choices.

A Story about Life Choices....

What are your life choices based on? Did you choose your career with guidance and prompting by your parents? Did you stay in a relationship because it was easier than starting over? Do you tolerate friends or family who are toxic to your wellbeing?

When he said to me that he feels like a pawn in everyone else's life, it told me much. Giving up your desires and convictions to please others or to make your life appear easier will never be the answer to achieving an existence you enjoy. He chose a career that was safe. It would give him the means that he needed to live comfortably; the comfort was external. He longed to be spending his days at a slower pace and putting his efforts into something very different.

When he was young his parents set him on a path that they felt was going to be secure and stable. He did not have much of a voice and followed the path they saw fit. He has great artistic talent, aspirations of being an artist, a starving artist if need be. His soul cried out to spend his days immersed in beauty and creating. He also began a relationship with someone who liked to be in control and dictate what his days look like. He followed a life pattern from feeling a level of subconscious comfort being raised by controlling parents. Despite the fact he wanted to be free to travel and see the world, he stayed in this relationship. Locked into a life he never envisioned for himself. He did this out of fear of displeasing someone he loved although he could never fully define the love. He did not have an interest in having children. He had children. He had a love for them but resented his partner for deceiving him and becoming pregnant. His life has become a vision of something he never chose for himself. He decided that he was going to live the life he envisioned. Having responsibilities from his choices, he wove the obligations of his current life into a new life of hope and excitement.

We worked on many thoughts, reactions, and emotional triggers. He was given the task to explore his voice, his desires. We focused on what happens when you discover your life is not what you would have chosen. He was given the permission to feel bitter, feel a loss, emptiness, and disappointment. We explored what occurs when you not only compromise the big life choices but also your personality. He learned who you become when you can never be "yourself". He discovered it was not too late to re-evaluate his choices, his consequences, and focus on aligning his life with his desires.

He worked very hard to move past the illusion of the "perfect life" that he never intended to create. He became honest with himself and extremely sincere with others. This was done by examining his reactions to situations and bringing integrity to the forefront. This life shift came over time but the confidence from having a voice arise from within helped him to shift his daily routine and his lifestyle to one that he chose and loved. He premiered his art in a prestigious forum just a few years after walking away from his unaligned life. He has used his art to reach the masses and has utilized his success to vastly improve his life.

Messages about Life Choices

Decisions.

Do you struggle to make decisions? Keep a coin handy. Toss it when you need help. Not because it will make the decision for you, but you will wish for one of the sides when it is in the air. There is your answer. If you don't make a wish, trust the toss.

Changes.

Most humans are not comfortable with change, we like to have patterns. We like to know what to expect. We are most relaxed when we fall back on our normal reactions. It is not abnormal to stay in negative places to avoid change. What if we looked at the truth about change? Nothing stays the same. Are you living in the past? Are you wishing for a life you had before or thought you had before this moment? What are the positive aspects of change? New opportunities? More freedom? Explore shifts you are facing and know change will not wait for your acceptance but that does not mean you cannot grant it.

Choose wisely.

Sadly, sometimes people do not love themselves enough at times to choose relationships wisely. Your job is not to fix or save anyone at the cost of you or your happiness. You should never feel "less than", disrespected, or used. You should not feel attacked or in pain when you are around your partner. Some basic rules in a relationship are honesty, loyalty, and respect. All the lust and attraction in the world means nothing if you do not respect yourself for making the decision to be with someone. Being with someone because it is "easier" will have the most difficult ending. Feeling safe, free, trusted, and loved just as you are may be the hallmarks to look for. It is important not to settle for anything less than what you deserve. Make sure you love yourself enough to know what you deserve.

Integrity.

Let us think about this little word with so much meaning behind it.

Explore yourself and the people in your life. What is your moral code? What reputation do you want to live with every day? Do you reside in truth?

If you strive to make your best choices and live an honest life, you can go to sleep at night with no regrets.

On the receiving end.

Problems come in when people in your life do not live with veracity and you are on the receiving end of being taken advantage of and underappreciated. The key is to love and value yourself, but it is still difficult to face other people's choices every day. How do you cope with this? People who live avoiding responsibility and truth, even when they do not seem to acknowledge their behaviors, have a pain inside you would never want. Deeply hurt people avoid living authentically. Send them love from the place within you that is whole. Go on your way. No other person's choices can hold you back.

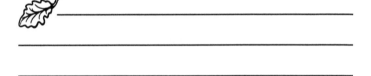

Listen Closely.

Having a strong relationship with yourself will allow you to pay attention to what you see, feel, and hear around and within you. We are all able to tap into our intuition at any time. You are getting universal messages of what is good for you, what the next step is on your path. Your mind may question or block what your intuition is telling you. It takes practice to learn what a message is from the energies around you versus your mind. If you have multiple signs of the same idea or thought repeatedly, chances are that is the universe trying to guide you. Step out of the craziness of your mind and everyday life and truly listen. Real signs come in the form of warm, loving, reassuring messages. Even if they are a "warning" they are a gentle nudge in another direction. Look for love, reassurance and repetitive positive energy and vibes. You are so capable of tuning in to a higher level if you let go of stress related to what you are sensing.

Comfort zone.

We pretend to trust what we can control, what we see on the surface of situations. If you move further away from what you can see and toward your inner self, that is where growth occurs. Happiness arises. Are you stuck in your comfort zone? Is it time to challenge your perspective? Ask yourself what benefit you get from staying comfortable. Sometimes that is the best we can do at any given time and that is ok, but when it is time to grow it is time to leave the feeling of comfort behind.

Nothing wrong.

There is nothing "wrong" with you. We are all living the human experience moving through different levels of growth. No situation or person is blocking you. You are in control of your life choices. You can control the steps you take toward becoming the healthiest version of you, based on what you think is healthy. No one else can define that for you. Challenge yourself every day to move through these steps. Love your life, it is the only one you have. Embrace yourself for all that is not wrong with you.

Honesty.

The ability to be honest, teach honesty, and embrace the truth is at the foundation of all relationships. Think of the emotions and situations that would be spared if people were simply honest. When people lie or deceive others, they are damaging others at their core. They are taking away the ability to trust, to want to build interpersonal relationships. The cruelest of it is when people do not have empathy for others. Consider the reasons people have that are completely invalid before they lie to someone. To protect them? To protect themselves? Honesty is always best. It may hurt, but dignity can be maintained, and people can move forward with a clear conscience. People will never be their authentic self if they lie to themselves or others.

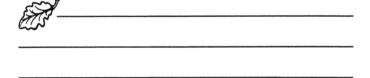

Priorities.

What is your calling? What makes your heart sing? When you focus on these areas, your joyful energy increases, which benefits everyone. Make choices that honor your priorities and support your life's mission. Despite what society says, your priorities are important and have meaning. They do not have to make sense to or live up to the expectations of others.

_____

_____

_____

Challenges

**Life is full of trials and tribulations.
How you face the situations you
choose and those just given to you
will dictate how you live your life.**

A Story about Challenges...

Everyone meets situations that they must handle physically, emotionally, or spiritually as they move through life. Some difficulties are a result of choices made. Some are out of our control. How you see challenges and plan to meet them is going to dictate your healing and recovery. Some people are inherently more prepared to deal with challenges. They see the positive side and value in overcoming situations. Others get stuck within the challenge. They must work diligently to maneuver through. Some feel as if they never move through, they just layer the experiences on top of each other until they become fully over extended emotionally.

She shared with me many stories of hardship. A difficult childhood riddled with abuse and neglect. A marriage that was similar. The loss of a child. Personal illness. The sudden passing of someone very important in her life. Yet, she was still standing. Still living her life to the best of her ability. She was seeking to shift her energy into a place where she felt peace. A place where she could move forward without regret of some choices, without resentment for the incidents that befell her.

We worked on living in the moment and releasing past experiences. Focusing on the now, only using the past as something to pull strength from. There was a new understanding of setting attainable goals for emotional understanding. Using role playing for situations that were to be expected and reframing the unexpected she was able to make it to a place of contentment. Challenges are on everyone's path. It is how you respond to them that will define their impact in your life.

She used her challenges in life to work with others. This is what moved her through the tough times and into much more content life. She took the skills she learned on her healing journey and passed them on to those who were ready to face the need to shift their lives. She attained a higher education in Psychology and her knowledge combined with life experience led her to become a leader in the field. She told me looking back at what she experienced it feels like a book about someone else's life now, a book that now touches her soul and gives her hope to grow further.

Messages about Challenges

Temporary.

Life is all about change. You and your world change daily, slowly turning in various directions. Focusing on living in the moment, as things are, will allow you to be truly alive. Dwelling on the past, yearning for who you once were, or wishing to go back to an old situation is not going to serve you. Fearing the future which you cannot control will not help you. Trust your path as it unfolds daily.

The only certainty in life is change. Embrace variations by uncovering your buried emotions, explore your experiences. Where can you see joy in this temporary moment?

_____

_____

_____

What you resist, persists.

A wonderful mantra for you as you move through life. So many emotions to contend with. So many ups and downs we are not trained or prepared for. Relationships, parenting, our own mental health. The biggest question is always "how". How do I make changes? What exactly do I "do"? You must actively work every day until your changes become habit. It is possible to break the cycles that you have created. It is worth the energy since your other option is staying in a negative place which takes just as much work.

Questions to ask yourself when issues arise.

Would I rather be right or at peace (external and internal conflicts)?

Am I living to my highest and honest potential (is my outer world aligned with my soul and calling)?

Am I living in the moment or am I pondering the past or fearing the future? (do I label myself as depressed/dwelling in the past or anxious/fearing the future)?

Am I allowing someone or something to victimize me? (are you using substances or being treated poorly in relationships? Are you being lied to or manipulated? Are you emotionally hurting others?)

Can I close my eyes at night knowing I am living honestly, cleanly, and with admirable intentions. Am I doing my best?

Identify your weaknesses, strengths, and goals. Get to work to make happiness, peace and love persist.

Cry.

Were you taught that if you cry you are weak? There is a physical and emotional purpose to crying, why else would we be able to cry? Crying releases stress hormones. If you continue to bottle up the emotions, you begin to have mental and physical blocks. Our society often teaches us that crying shows a lack of control. This is amiss. Crying is a way to show strength. Once you cry, your mind is free to solve problems, to heal. You become weak emotionally and physically when you cannot express emotion. Embrace those tears and explore the emotion to release your inner angst. Support your children, partner, friends when they cry. They will be stronger for it and you will become more emotionally healthy.

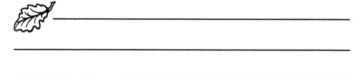

Storms in life.

What is your latest storm? Part of life for everyone is riding them out. Big or small, what is your storm making way for? What is it teaching you? What door may it open? What is it encouraging you let go of? It is wonderful when life flows along peacefully but if you expect the weather to always be sunny you will be disappointed for sure. Showing up for each day and knowing it will bring its blessings and challenges is a positive plan. It is all about having both your sunglasses and rain gear with you every day.

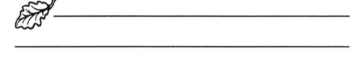

_____

_____

Work in progress.

Life is a work in progress. No one fits precisely in your shoes. Meet your feelings and challenges head on. Whatever bandage you are putting on your problems need to be ripped off to let the trouble really heal. If you are suffering with depression, anxiety, anger issues, even substance abuse; these are not the problem. Your unresolved emotions are the challenge. Explore beneath the bandage, seek help, and investigate ways to attain emotional health. The covers will fall off, your life will improve, and the people in your circle will feel the ripple effect.

Holding on can cause more damage than letting go.

People hold on to so many painful things, negative relationships, toxic memories, self-defeating behaviors. When you are fighting yourself to continue to hold on, picture two hands. One holding a rope so tight the hand is red and in pain. Picture the free, healthy hand open to bringing in the positive once you let go with the other hand and use both hands to take hold of freedom. Think of the great things on the other side once use your strength to grab all that you deserve. New opportunities, new connections. Let go and live in peace.

Surrender.

We all want answers. We strive to understand why we feel the way we do. We ask what would make someone else have certain behaviors. What if you surrendered to the unknown and trusted that things are working out the way they are supposed to for you? The lessons that fall into your path do not need to be controlled or understood completely. The things that happen to you and others are just that- things that happen. The only control you have in life are the decisions you initially make and the response to your decisions in the end. A huge part of surrender is doing your best, being true to yourself like being honest, fair, and working to your highest potential. Accept what follows. Remember that you can never control anyone else. Not your friends, family, co-workers, spouse, children. You must trust that you communicated your needs in the fairest way and then you sit back and surrender. When you surrender, you are free.

Struggles.

What is your struggle in life? What do you wish most to overcome? Every day we wake up with the opportunity to face what gives us angst in this life. Meet it head on, bravely. Make the difficult choices to endure through your day with purpose. Try to stop just "surviving ". You are slowly overcoming your difficulties, that is what life is about. Take the challenges unique to you; observe, accept, respect, and move through them. Review each accomplishment and be proud of yourself. The keys are to love yourself no matter what, be pleased with yourself always, and look within, not to others or external rewards for worth. Explore your worth to this world. What do your struggles offer you and others that walk this path with you? Every little bit of peace you feel no matter how small offers a smidgen of your soul healing and growth. Love life, be thankful for every breath, and take nothing for granted.

_____

_____

_____

Take your time.

Patience. What does that mean to you? Have you been asking for help, praying, wondering when you will feel better or get to where you want to be in life? Patience is the ability to trust your journey and fate while working toward your goals of living in peace every day. Life takes work and persistence, the drive to create the best version of you and time to see yourself bloom. Be patient with yourself and the world surrounding you.

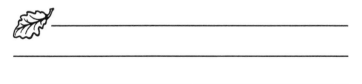

Fear.

Fear is your mind's response to uncomfortable emotions. Nothing else.

Yes, fear has its rightful place if there is a logical imminent threat to your life. Fear may also come from the unknown when a challenging situation arises. How do you help yourself when a fear develops? Ask questions of yourself. Is my life in danger right at this moment? If so, embrace that fear and try to save yourself. Or am I fearing something I cannot control? Go deeper to what your underlying emotion is related to the fear. Bring it to the surface as many times as you must. Acceptance will neutralize it over time. Never avoid what causes you fear if you want to overcome it. This behavior will create stronger pathways in your mind that help you to build on the fear, to become frightened of the apprehension, thus, never let you be free of it.

We learn from what we least desire.

As we move through life, we get very frustrated with others at times because of their behavior, beliefs, and general way they go about life. It seems the more frustrated we are, the more these people come into our paths. Why? You could just be noticing it more or it could be the lessons that you need to learn in life to help you to be calmer, happier, and more in touch with yourself. Think about what you can learn from every experience you encounter. What are behaviors of the people and how are things unfolding around you? Why are your frustration buttons being pushed? This exploration may just be exactly what you need to learn more about yourself.

_____

_____

_____

Growing pains.

Even when living a painful existence your mind will fight to keep you in a familiar place. When we are growing psychologically and moving to a higher emotional level more aligned with our souls as each day passes, it can hurt. It can cause our minds to fight back. Create scary thoughts. This is just your thinking mind trying to protect you from the unknown. Your spirit will win if you allow it. How do you go through it? Let yourself feel all of those "growing pains". Remorse, fear, shame, and anger will soon turn into contentment, pride, confidence, and love if you let your outer life align with your inner callings. You are worth so much. You have an abundance of wonderful things to offer yourself and this world. Step up and do the hard work to discover your worth. The growing pains are always worth the life expansion in the end.

_____

_____

_____

Anxiety.

If you have pervasive worry or anxiety you may be trying to avoid the unknown, change, or uncertainty. The irony is that the behaviors you use to stop or avoid feelings of anxiety are not protecting you at all. They are breaking you down emotionally and physically. If you are not truly living life and are tired of surviving instead of thriving, the good news is that you can stop using safety behaviors that support your worry. How? When the anxious or debilitating thoughts come in, replace them with thoughts of support and compassion for yourself. Offer yourself the option to explore anxiety and confront it. Using rational thinking to balance the anxious thoughts will help you to accept situations with ease. Use the idea of possibility versus probability. Can anything happen at any time? Of course. Is it most likely to happen? Usually not. Another way to examine anxiety is to think through your life. How many of the things that you worried about happened the way you thought they would? Have you had times when things you never expected happened well before anything you were worrying about? This is a fact of life to teach us to accept what is.

_____

_____

Free time.

Some people look at free time as wasted time. What if free time is a gift? What if this time is given to you to reconnect to your family? Or to work on things that you need to fix in your life. What if this is time in your life that you can have uninterrupted peace? Spend time with your family, learn something new, or work on yourself. Embrace free time to stay connected in your life to yourself and the world around you.

_____

_____

Worries.

What are your worries right now? What are you focusing on? The key to managing worries is to remind yourself that you are always protected by the supportive energy around you, and all is happening in perfect order.

Trust in the plan. Stay in the moment. Despite feeling out of control at times, you can count on all events happening for a reason and for your personal growth. Take one day at a time. Worrying never solves a problem.

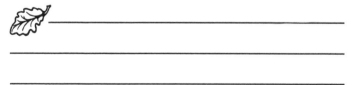
_____

_____

_____

Overcoming difficulties.

We all have difficulties and struggles every day. Even the most optimistic people carry the burdens of everyday life. Some have challenges that seem insurmountable. The way that you view the battles is what will dictate how you handle them. Do you take your troubles in and fight them? Refuse to accept them? Or do you let them flow through you like an ocean wave? Do you ask, "what am I feeling underneath this"? "What can I accept and learn from this"? Think of the hundreds of battles, challenges, and traumas that you have faced and overcame. You are still here, nothing has beat you yet. Today- smile, stand tall, and open your arms to difficulties with the knowledge that you have what it takes to handle it all.

Your soul knows.

If you are feeling anxiety, depression, grief, or rage it most often comes from the lack of understanding and acceptance of yourself. Try to avoid letting your mind continually get the better of you. How? Take the moment you are in and accept it fully, moving into the next and things will flow as they should. There is no good or bad, there just "is". There is no past and no future, only right now. You know what to do. Quiet the noise and put each moment in front of you, one at a time.

Slow down. Breath and free yourself from concerns.

_____

_____

_____

Emotions

**Human emotions are the barometer of life.
They help people to know what is needed
to focus on to keep moving forward.**

A Story about Emotions....

Many people view being strong as the result of how much you can avoid both positive and negative emotions in life. If you show any reaction that would display weakness, it may indicate you cannot handle life. Crying in some societies is frowned upon. Parents tell little children to stop crying, to toughen.up, to stop being a baby. Even showing positive emotion at times may draw criticism. Someone may be labeled as a narcissist or being unrealistic in life. There are many repercussions to avoiding emotion. Healthy people embrace all their emotions and work to understand them, regardless of societal pressures.

He grew up in a family with a dad who was tough, he wanted his boys to play sports and show no pain. He wanted them to take emotional hits and have no reaction. He took cues from the tough, popular kids in school who never let any weakness show. Now he is an adult who has spent his life hiding how he feels. He does this out of fear of disappointing people if he displays what he feels is weakness.

The problem he identified to me was that his lack of revealing emotion has led to a very disconnected relationships with his partner, children, and friends. He is by nature a sensitive man. He was a sensitive child too. The expectation to be strong and not respond emotionally has led him to be unsure of himself and his relationships. He also talked about feeling shame when he experienced sadness or pain even to himself. Working on the idea of shame was a difficult task. Thinking about the fact that a valid reason to feel shame would result from someone intentionally acting in a way is morally or ethically inappropriate was enlightening to him. That idea alone helped him to understand that emotions are not intentional. They are a person's reaction to an experience. They cannot be controlled, only worked with to be expressed. The power is only in the reaction to the feeling.

Relearning how to experience emotion and showing his sentiments to himself and others was the goal.

To do this, every aspect of his life was examined, and he gave himself permission to feel and show emotion in the moments that were most difficult. He had to literally learn something that is best taught to children: identifying and reacting appropriately to sensations that are felt after an experience. Although this was uncomfortable to work on, the new normal and his ability to be his true self in relationships healed many years of pain. He and his partner gained a deeper understanding of each other. His children became free to show emotion and have healthy discussions with him about how they were feeling. The home environment became a safe place to land on the roughest days. His drive to heal sent a ripple effect of acceptance and love through everyone in his life. If he decided to never approach the toughest challenge he faced his whole life, he would have missed out on the beauty in himself and all that he has to offer to the people in his life.

Messages about Emotions

All is good.

Now is the time to shed away hate, disappointment, and negativity. Usher in a new perspective that achieves your highest good. There are abundant joys and beauty all around you. Look at the world with honesty and love in your heart. Opening your eyes and seeing through the challenges will help you to realize how wonderful life is. Allow yourself to see truth and your authentic feelings.

Peace.

How do people go about finding peace within? How do you achieve real and lasting peace? Through passion, appreciation of one's self, and of the positive things surrounding you. Let go of culpability, fears, and shame. Focus on devotion to yourself and all of those around you. Look for the big and small achievements, from the smile on a stranger's face to the excitement of a big goal met. You have so many reasons to feel peace, it just takes effort sometimes to refocus the negative within and around us to see it. Make a list in your mind of what brings you peace. What within you represents peace? What do others in your life do that creates harmony? Negative thoughts will try to move in, say no thank you and refocus. Setting your goal of focusing on synchronization will bring you great joy. It is a daily practice, which is sometimes not easy, but if you reorient your thinking, you will feel the results.

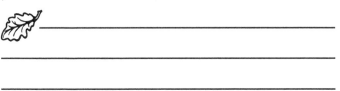

_____

_____

_____

Enthusiasm.

Passion, what a great experience in life. One that many of us are lacking. The energy is around you right now to support enthusiasm in your life. How can you tap into it? Listen to the messages you hear and see that are supportive of a spark; it is there waiting for you to see and act upon. Look for what brings you joy and contentment. Focus on those things, not in the negative that swirls around us. If you keep your eye and mind on what makes you happy, more contentment will come. Your focus is your decision. The universe always puts great things on your path. Passion is one of them. You deserve to be happy and at peace and to be in love with your life.

_____

_____

_____

Mindset.

Mindset is everything. Changing how you experience life changes your life experience. Although it may not come naturally for you, you can start to slowly change your thoughts and reactions to situations. What you water will grow. Make sure you are feeding a healthy mind, body, and soul by checking on your view of all that you encounter. Use a checklist about what is beneficial to you and what is not. When you face a challenge use a number scale one to ten to check in truly and accurately on yourself. If something feels overwhelming it is a ten or a five? Often you will find you are in a better head space than you thought.

_____

_____

Valor.

There is so much going on in the world. There is always support from positive sources. Look to the energy around you. Look within at what you have survived through up to this point in life. Pain, joy, suffering: you are still standing. You have the emotional wounds to show for it all. Behind those battle scars you have strength, perseverance, and purpose. Focus on courage, the fact that your energy and soul are still here and ready to fight for yourself and others. Go out into the world today strong and determined. Always remember that no situation is permanent; brighter days are ahead and a stronger "you" will be there to live them. Look to all the other souls who are helping, loving, yearning for better. Collective courage will rise the energy vibration of humanity. Stay strong, fearless, and courageous.

Benevolence.

We are often challenged to use compassion. We have fights within and with others that we do not know we are fighting or are not sure why. Compassion is challenging beliefs and emotions to rise to your best level. The next time you face an internal or external problem ask yourself the best way to have compassion. That will give you the room to breathe and move forward. Everyone wants to be loved, accepted, and belong. Walking in someone else's shoes and treating others as you would like to be treated are good ways to start on a compassionate path. Even if the shoes and path are your own.

What to quit today.

Quit living in the past, pleasing everyone, trying to conform, wondering if you are worth it, beating yourself up, being unhappy for someone else to be happy, thinking too much. Time to quit.

Tolerance.

Patience. A difficult idea for most. What does patience mean to you? Do you feel you are a patient person? Do you want to be more tolerant or is this something you despise to hear from others? The concept of patience is an interesting one.

If you notice, the most serene people are those who are first accepting of themselves. When you at least appreciate your struggles, it is much easier to acknowledge the world around you, slow down and have tolerance for others and the flow of life. Everyone has internal wounds. Next time you are feeling impatient remember that the path you are on is exactly where you need to be. Take a breath, slow down, look to acknowledge the situation or other person's behavior and practice patience.

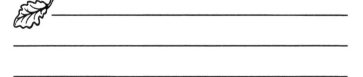

There is always a reason.

There is a reason you are in your current situation. It is for your own good, so use it to grow. Is your child pushing your buttons, are you stuck in traffic, is a friend or relative being intolerable? Look beneath these outward annoyances. Your child is trying to learn, maybe being stuck in traffic is the universe's way of placing you where you need to be. Perhaps your friend needs some love and support. Tolerance is a wonderful emotion to dive into. Today and moving forward, go with love and understanding for yourself and others.

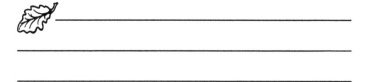

_____

_____

_____

Inspiration.

There is great importance in naming your motivation when you are in situations.

Create your moment. What is your motivation to react in the way you are responding? Are you protecting yourself? Responding out of the need to be right about something? Are you growing? What are your goals? Every moment carries with it an opportunity to raise your game, to achieve the best you. The new day brings the chance to drive toward inner peace and external glory. To grow in life, to become our authentic selves, we must be inspired. We ought to think and process our action and reactions. That is where you find motivation to work with your inspiration.

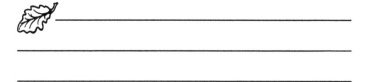

_____

_____

_____

Introspection.

Sensitivity is a beautiful thing if it is accepted. We are taught to fight it, to push it away and deal with everything we experience and feel no matter how much we struggle internally. It is time to honor your sensitivity and express it through acceptance. We were not made to be mighty iron soldiers. We are human. We all have feelings and emotions that we experience. Pushing sentiments away creates physical and emotional challenges. It is important to feel, laugh, cry, have joy and hurt when you need to. No longer cast a shadow on your feelings. Live them with confidence. Sensitivity and introspection should be honored.

Validation vs. invalidation.

This is a difficult concept in our society for a few reasons. People want to ignore emotional responses as much as possible, so they rarely validate their own or anyone else's. This leads at times to the inability for people to stay in relationships or even raise healthy children. The "suck it up" mentality needs to be dispelled. This does not mean having unaccountability for your actions; it means owning all your choices and responses to them. We need people to care for our feelings and we absolutely need to acknowledge and validate our own.

Let life flow.

There are no "good" or "bad" feelings. We name them based on how we are supposed to react. Most often bury the negative and cover it with poor coping skills. And when things are "good" we breeze through without appreciating or valuing the moment. It takes practice to let things flow and accept the moment for whatever it is. Living in the past, fearing the future, denying the now- all recipes for pain. You have what you need within the moment and within yourself.

Happiness

What if you could be happy and live in harmony? What if you have all the tools and ability to find your bliss? There are many ways to find happiness and explore a positive and exciting life.

A Story about Happiness...

"I just want to be happy". This is a sentence that I hear many times a week. My response is always the same. You can choose happiness at any moment. Although this may seem like an insurmountable feat for some, there are people who do not have to choose. There are a lucky few who live in that place by the nature of their spirit.

She was a perfect example of this. Brimming with joy, she was the image of all the steps one would take to seek, feel, and spread bliss. Some people have a natural energy that is aligned with the positive, with seeing the good and all of the enjoyment life has to offer.

She had this. With a diagnosis of cancer at a young age, she was challenged to look for hope. She was given the gift of learning that life is not eternal. When asked how her day was the answer was always the same. "It's a wonderful and perfect day"! With a smile on her face she would always leave people with genuine kind words and a feeling of hope.

Her biggest challenge was living among others who are unable to see the beauty of life. She would feel angry and an urgency to respond to many people in her life who she felt continually tried to bring her down. She set a goal to have a deeper understanding of the lens of life others looked through. She realized that these people were often not intentionally attacking her personality. They were living their own reality. People usually put little to no thought into understanding how they are being perceived by others.

Once she had a richer view of the dynamics of the people in her life, she was more able to accept the view through their eyes. This helped her to continue her life of happiness without feeling challenged by others.

What can we learn from people who embrace all that comes their way? What is the secret to seeing the good in life and accepting what happens? How do we look though the eyes of a child with wonder and excitement as we move through our adult lives? It can be done. Your energy can shift to a place that makes you want to live each day to the fullest despite your innate views of the world.

Messages about Happiness

Contentment.

What does happiness mean to you? There are always parts of life where pleasure can be found. Is it human nature to take things for granted? Does personal life experience, society or just who you are as a person lead you to be blind to the happiness that surrounds you? The key to learning to find your peace in life comes in two parts. First step is becoming content with yourself. Truly accepting and being in love with yourself is the key to enjoying life. Next, making decisions that are good for you. This entails doing whatever makes you feel at peace that puts you in a positive frame of mind. Your actions will lead to contentment if they are healthy and allow you to grow as a person. Explore your definition and vision of happiness. What are the aspects that you use to describe being content?

_____

_____

_____

Building blocks.

Watch the stories that your mind creates. All unhappiness truly comes from what your mind generates. What you say to yourself about situations produce your response. You have the power to change your life with your inner dialogue. Spend one day paying attention to the stories that you tell in your mind, observing the moments and deciding how happy or unhappy you really are. What can you look at differently today to increase your level of acceptance and joy?

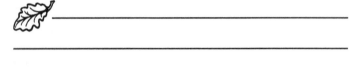

Create a life worth living.

Self-love and your choices are the keys to a fruitful life. Messy things like experiences and emotions can get in the way. Refusing to be the victim of anything or anyone will get you further. You have all the tools within to create a life worth living. You build your life; no one else can do that for you. The opinions and actions of other people are irreverent. They have no true impact on your life, they have a perceived impact when you take them and create your stories and identity around them. Live honestly and in truth with yourself and everything else will fall into place. Build a life you do not need to run from but long to run towards.

You have a Purpose.

People often ask what their purpose is in life. It is what you experience every day. You play a role in the web of this world. Every decision you make creates a ripple effect and impacts someone else's life. Even at times when you feel that you are contributing nothing of importance. Look at each part of your daily life, the little things. Your interaction with a stranger. A smile for someone as they walk by. That could be the moment that person changes their life from that gesture of kindness. Or your lack of caring, your negative response to someone. That action could lead that person on a path of unhappiness for the day. Take your purpose seriously. You are important.

Wellness.

How do you define wellness? Your mental health is the key to your overall health. Positive mental health depends how able we are to take in life. People fight themselves and those around them in various ways most of the day. How would your life look if you worked on acknowledging everything and everyone as they are right now? Including yourself? You can always have plans to better your situation or to be a support for someone else but think of your life in this moment. How many issues are going on that you would like to accept? How would your wellness be positively impacted if you went through everyday focusing on what is best for your mental health, on what truly matters?

_____

_____

_____

Accept.

Acceptance does not mean loving a situation, it means letting it be until it changes. Worry, anxiety, and stress are most always related to lack of control. Looking at what the options are for your responses to people and situations while accepting what is happening is the key to managing any condition. What would happen if you gave up control? What if you were to accept life and people as they are right now. You, your partners "stuff", your children's challenges? Everyone is on a journey that needs no definition or control from anyone else. Release yourself from the need to manage every moment and watch how things change for you.

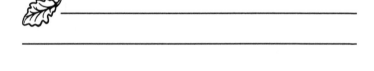

The right words.

Using the right words in your life when you talk to others or about yourself is imperative to achieving positive mental wellbeing. Try to reframe your conversations that you have about yourself day by day and see how much more content you feel. You are capable of retraining and rewiring your mind. Practice being unapologetic for who you are. When you are struggling with emotions or physical pain, try rewording your conversations in and outside of your mind. Do you have physical pain? Instead of describing it as horrible or stabbing or crushing, try for example, "I am not feeling as comfortable as I like". You mind will hear the word comfortable and relax your body instead of hearing "horrible" and tense up. Emotional pain? Instead of saying "I am so stressed, I can't go on" try, "I am not feeling as relaxed as I would like to be, but I will feel better soon". It is not lying to yourself or saying things that are not true, it is healthy alternative to a negative focus and will have a direct impact on what response your body and mind has.

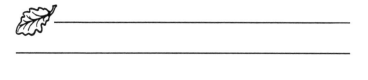

_____

_____

_____

Joy.

What are you waiting for? You have all the ingredients for happiness at your fingertips right now. No one and nothing is responsible for you feeling happy. Only you. It all comes from within. This is a difficult idea in our society. We look to other people, money and even addictions to hide behind and pretend what brings us "happiness". Yes, having financial means makes life more comfortable and yes, being around dysfunctional people is difficult to stop at times. It is not easy to change your mindset but look for the truth within. Your joy will come from you being truthful with yourself and working on your responses to your life situations.

_____

_____

_____

Choice.

People fall victim to circumstances and other people. Always remember you have a choice in every situation. It may be a difficult one, but you always can choose to appreciation over everything else. Look at your living situation, the people around you, your job, how you parent, what kind of friend you are.

Are you happy with your choices? Do you feel a sense of love for yourself and peace within? Are you being honest with yourself? What can you adjust so that you create your own happiness? Have gratitude for life and your place in the world. Choose wisely to create the life you want.

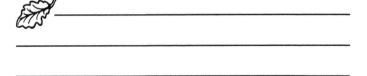

In the moment.

Embrace what you are doing fully in every moment. Be it something enjoyable, mundane, or painful. Releasing the fear of what is to come will allow you to enjoy your life as it is. Take mental pictures, use your senses to fully take in the moments as they come. Focus on sounds and smells. Look at the colors surrounding you. Observe the people around you. Look at who they really are. What emotions do you share with others? When you realize that you are connected to the world you will appreciate the moments more. Feel excitement for your life and experiences. Live fully in your environment. Enjoy your moments; they are what create your life.

_____

_____

Your future is now.

The only future you have is the very next breath you take. Let go of planning and worrying. It is all useless. You cannot change the past and cannot control your future. Do what you love every second you can and enjoy following your heart as it leads you in the right direction.

You are the project.

People spend their lives trying to achieve "success". The right school, right career, right mate; what about you? One major job in life that people have is undoing the wrong choices or poor decisions they make in life. If you are wondering why the job does not feel right, you cannot make ends meet, or you are in a less than exciting relationship maybe it is because you have some work on yourself to do. Your feelings about your worth will dictate what you seek. Getting to know who you really are apart from everything else is imperative. When a person is emotionally healthy, they make sound choices, and their lives are easier, happier. There is no more noble project in life than you.

_____

_____

_____

Gifts from beyond.

We need to be receptive and willing to receive what good is all coming our way. Focus is best to be left on the blessings we have and experiences that will invite further gifts in. What are you grateful for today? What are you willing to open yourself up to? Do you believe in universal energy guiding you? Do you feel that fate is real? There are no coincidences.

_____

_____

_____

Gratitude.

Humans will focus on almost anything else but being a friend to ourselves.

If everyone started with a few healthy mental practices a day, people would be able to accomplish so much more for themselves and in society. A happy self is a productive self. Gratitude practice is a sound, easy way to shift your view of the world. As soon as you open your eyes every morning, think of, or even better say, out loud, three things in your life you are grateful for. As this becomes a habit, add more thoughts throughout the day of gratitude. The more you focus on the good, the less room you will have to hold on to stress.

8

Action

**Acting in your life means moving
toward your goals with purpose.
Making steps to improve your situation
will empower you to live fully.**

A Story about Action....

Addiction. It is something that many people struggle with
or have experienced through being exposed to others
in life. Compulsion toward substances or behaviors has
much to do with unresolved emotions coming to fruition.
Thanks to modern science we do know that one may be
predisposed to addiction genetically, but does that alone
determine the decision to walk that path completely?
What is the trigger to introduce one's self to substances
or risky behaviors? Often it is to dull the senses, to have
fun to be accepted to a group or simply out of curiosity.
What drives people to continue the use or behavior?
This is where the sensation of limiting emotion may
come in. People who struggle with acknowledging or
sharing feelings and emotions may use substances to bury
uncomfortable feelings, to dull their senses or to escape
from reality.

He had multiple concerns. Struggling with interpersonal relationships, withdrawing from himself and others. Avoiding conflict and using substances to "numb" himself from life day after day. Taking action to resolve challenges was not something that was appealing or easy for him to do. He got to the point where life was not worth living in his eyes any longer.

He was successful in life, to the outsider. No one knew how much he was struggling. He was at a crossroads. The choices had to be made to move toward life or his demise.

Action does not have to be sweeping and fast. It does not have to be successful every time. Acting happens in single moments. Looking at every day and each emotion behind behaviors takes time and energy. Often with addiction there needs to be multifaceted help for people. Looking at the basic beginning point of agreeing to act on behalf of oneself is the first step. He did this. He took the measures to replace negative behaviors, feelings, and reactions with constructive pursuits. He set up a plan of action he worked on replacing old behaviors with exciting new opportunities. Every small achievement was celebrated, and life shifted. There were setbacks but with the plans in place to get back on the path to health, he made it.

Five years have passed, and he is not looking back to that place where he once was. He continues to learn and practice good physical and emotional health. To him, life is good. He found his worth and found peace.

Messages about Action

Walk away.

Today is your day. You owe the world nothing, especially your unrest. Protect yourself, set boundaries, and be set free. Move into this day with self-respect and self-confidence. Distance emotionally from any person or experience that does not improve your life or state of mind. It is not your job to be less than all that you truly are. It is not your duty to lose yourself on behalf of others. Think about the relationships you have with yourself and others. Do you need to walk away from anything or anyone? Walking away is not failing; it is winning.

_____

_____

_____

It is in your response.

Think of situations in your life that bother you. What triggers your responses? People spend time being annoyed but not making any plans to manage emotions. When you are in the same frustrating situations everyday with people or your choices and it feels like a surprise every day, it may be time to ask why. A strategy to work on your reaction is to role play what you know is coming in your life day to day. Plan your reaction instead of being reactive. Once you honestly analyze what you are doing and why, it is easier to simplify your emotional response and align it to your goals.

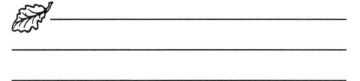

_____

_____

Everything is temporary.

Everything and everyone is temporary in life. Including you. Nothing will be in your life forever. Each moment and experience is important for what it is.

The only thing that is certain is change. Why do we try so hard to hold on to everything knowing none of it is permanent? Security? Safety? It is all an illusion.

Unease and despair, frustration and sadness are all results of deceptions we create to feel in control. Next time you are feeling upset examine why. Can you control what may happen at all? If you can, take control and make the decisions that suit you.

If it is out of your control you have the power to let it go. Think of the hours and hours wasted of your life on feeling "bad". How has this improved your life? When are you going to make the changes to enjoy your existence? Live. Let live. Love.

_____

_____

_____

Self-Care.

Take care of yourself first. So many people fight this. People emotionally feel, "I don't deserve to worry about myself, that is selfish, I don't matter as much as my family". These ideas come from learning false, flawed coping skills. The concept that your only role in life is to take care of everything and everyone but yourself is not productive. If you do not make time to feel emotionally strong and happy, you cannot help others to feel that way. As the saying goes, you cannot pour from an empty glass. If you truly love "your people" you must love yourself, so others get the best and healthiest version of you.

It is your life.

You will find your peace when you realize you do not have much influence in life except in the decisions that you make every day. Even the smallest of choices can change your path drastically. To make the best determinations for you, first define your goals, morals, and values. Your choices will be much easier to make if you know what they are based on. For example, if you know you want to be treated with fairness and integrity you can decide if the life situations you are in fit your desires. If you truly want to be strong and care for yourself, you can make plans that match those goals. The key is that you do not stray from your values. Hold true to what you want in your life.

Instincts.

Instincts are internal decision-making tools that help you to move through your life. We are all intertwined and play a role in the world. Everyone has a purpose. Using your instincts to decide how you fit into the world will help you to take care of yourself. Listen to your impulses. What are they telling you? Think before you act. Take pause to make sure your actions are guided by instincts not knee-jerk reactions. Have confidence in yourself, be patient, and trust your intuition.

Be gentle.

Be gentle with yourself. People do not know your story and you do not know theirs. No one can dictate how you view yourself based on their reactions toward you. Stand strong in your beliefs, walk with certainty, and go easy on yourself. You are no better and no less than any other person. Go out there and live in your own truth. Be gentle and at peace with yourself.

Take flight.

It is a time for renewal and growth. Let go of the old and welcome the new. Release anguish, sorrow, irritation, and old stories you replay over and over that keep you from harmony and rest. It is time to give yourself permission to live, to fly, to feel, not think or reason your way through your days. Move into each moment with excitement and anticipation of what good may come. The past is gone, it is irrelevant to who you are right now. The future truly does not exist for anyone for certain. Go out into the world, fearless and spread your wings. That idea you have for trying something new is brought to you by a higher source. Listen to it. You only have this moment, this breath, this very minute to live in. Put your focus on adoring yourself, enjoying what you love, and everything will fall into place.

Action.

Doing the work on yourself will always pay off. Be it mental, emotional, or physical. There is always work to be done and rewards to achieve.

There is nothing you cannot face, overcome, or accomplish. It is not all luck; it is focus and action. What step can you take today to improve your life? What does action look like to you?

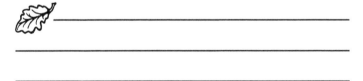

Write your own story.

You are not your life experiences. You are not your old worries. You are not your parents or siblings. You are not a victim. Stop beating yourself up and trying to control things you cannot. Respect yourself. Move into your life, and write your own narrative. You can take all that you have experienced and map your journey moving forward. Your life story can be rewritten and revised as often as you like.

Whatever you do not change, you choose.

It is all about choices. Whenever you feel wronged, ask what part your choices have played in it. Sometimes things happen that are unexpected but most of our lives are created by what we choose. Where you live, who your partner is, how people are allowed to treat you, how healthy you are, what you do for a living, how you look at life; all choices. If you chose to stay in a situation than you need to own it and make the best of it. If you need help to make better choices, own that, and act. It may not be easy, but neither is staying unhappy.

You are the master of your world, not other people.

People try to fix or change others as a condition for being in a relationship, friendship, or even maintaining a familial connection. This will never work. You must make the choice to accept people just as they are. Your control in a relationship is only your thoughts and behaviors. Define the type of people you want in your life. What are you willing to accept and at what cost? The choice is always yours. If someone is not fitting into the vision of your best life because you cannot change your reactions to their behavior, it may be time to set yourselves free of each other.

_____

_____

_____

Pretend you chose this moment.

The key to all happiness is acceptance. Approval of your present moment, every decision you make, and the repercussions of the choices you make. Recognition of the fact that you cannot control others or many situations in life. Acknowledgement of how you feel emotionally and/or physically. The more you oppose anything, the more it shall endure. The quicker you to learn to accept and take responsibility for your decisions, the more content you will be in the moment. It takes practice to reframe your thoughts, but it can be done.

It is all clear.

A sound daily practice is to set your intentions clearly and move forward. It is important to focus on what is immediately in front of you, not what has passed or what may come. Feelings of remorse and sadness can come from living in the past. Worry and angst can derive from thoughts about what may come. Look positively toward your goals for this day and gently through the looking glass of the rest of your life with no expectations of control.

Victory.

Today have faith in the unknown. You have been working on being the best "you" for yourself and everyone in your life even if you do not feel like you have. Accept where you are, look at your achievements and what you would like to move toward. We are all "works in progress". Go easy on yourself, rejoice in the victories, no matter how small, and keep moving forward. You are more successful than you think.

Courage.

It takes courage to thrive under pressure. Even if it is just the everyday pressure of living. Be the role model for yourself and the people in your life. Do the best that you can and aim to allow yourself to feel strong and courageous. Let any feelings of shame, worry, dissatisfaction, sadness, and angst fall aside. Let today show your confidence, joy, peace, happiness, and strength. Choose what will make your day bright. Every day that you make this choice, your life will become better. Have the courage to lead yourself and others on the path to enjoying life.

Healing

**Healing in life takes many forms.
Emotional, mental, physical. You can
heal your life whenever you are ready.**

A Story about Healing....

One of the biggest joys is working with people and witnessing the healing that takes place in lives over time. Many people resist change; they are uncertain about how to heal. Once someone learns ways to find peace, they are inspired to get stronger and embrace life more each day. There is no certain way or rule for healing. Every person must embrace what works for them.

She was very reluctant to listen to the ideas for making positive changes. She fought her own intuition, my guidance, and the path that sat in front of her. But she always returned, always wanted to keep working. The largest block for her was the lack of trust in the world that plagued her, the void she felt inside. She sensed a weakness within, an inability to heal herself. The breakthrough happened when she found love for herself, when she could finally look in a mirror into her the eyes and say, "I love you".

It took time and patience with herself. She became open to using healing practices. When we look at complete wellness, we think of physical, emotional, and spiritual healing. Humans are multifaceted. We are not simple beings. To heal, all aspects of us need to be aligned with positive intentions. There are many modalities for healing. It is important to encourage people to explore all that is available in the world that will help with healing. Traditional medicine and doctors help with alleviating symptoms of what ails. Alternative medicine and practices often consider the whole being. A small sample of practices to explore that are outside of the average visit to a doctor are working with Naturopathic Doctors, having acupuncture, taking part in hypnosis, seeking counseling, or practicing physical activities like yoga and energy healing. All of these modalities are available to people who want to explore possibilities for healing. The approach for mind, body, and soul healing will result in positive life satisfaction for most who take that path.

There are no limits to the happiness and joy that people can find in life. A focus on healing and growth will take you on a peaceful and successful journey.

She decided to seek help from alternative sources. She found much peace in bringing her mind, body, and spirit into alignment. Moving forward she decided to increase her education and became a Naturopathic Doctor. She moved from being uncertain and feeling broken to being successful, educated, and a healer to others. Sometimes the best path to self-healing is helping others.

Messages about Healing

Energy clearing.

Energy surrounds all of us. People take in energy all day. When you absorb other people's energy and it combines with your own it is important that you manage it within your body and mind. Mediate or concentrate on moving the energy through your body. When you go to sleep, or at any time in the day, take a break, picture loving energy moving up through your body, clearing any toxic energy. Picture it leaving your body. Clear your mind. Breathe in positive loving energy. Release toxic energy.

Relief.

We all need healing in our lives. Remember that the supportive verve is all around you. It may not come from other people. It comes from a universal energy and from within. What do you need to heal? Losses? Feelings of inadequacy? Failures? The good news is that none of these things can really hurt you if you change your perspective. Yes, the loss of people and parts of your life that you love is very hurtful, sad, and at times, near impossible to bear. What if you reminded yourself of what you gained from the people in your life, from your experiences? What if you moved forward with gratitude and joy for having another day to find peace through living? It is all in your hands to embrace a little bit at a time. Be proud of little steps you take to feel comfort. Relief comes from acceptance.

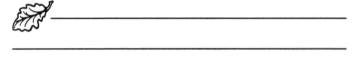

Quietness.

Now is a time for quietness and self-reflection. It is very important that you keep yourself grounded. Stay close to your own heart. Surround yourself with peace and things that bring you joy. Retreat from conflict. It will not benefit you to try and be heard right now. Take time off. Breathe, find what makes your heart sing. Now is a great time to practice being your own best friend.

Tenderness.

Be gentle with yourself. Take it easy. Give yourself a break. Clear your emotions and relax. Allow yourself to cry, laugh, be at peace. Decide what is good for you today, no one else. It is okay to take care of you, you truly do not owe anyone anything. You owe yourself peace. Find your calm today by being tender with yourself.

Cleaning.

It is a good time to clean out the old and make room for the new. Both in your surroundings and within yourself. Release what no longer serves you: Items, fears, negative thoughts, and energies. At the end of each day relax into the new freedom you created.

Breathing through it.

This is a reminder to pay attention to your breath. In times of stress and emotional discord, your body and soul need you to be mindful of your breathing so that you can relax. To become physically and mentally present take three mindful, full, calm breaths throughout each day whenever you can. This will bring focus to the present, oxygenate your body, and help you to feel much more in the moment. Use your breath to remind you to relax and focus on being well.

Power.

We all have supportive vitality around us. At times when we feel that the world and our minds are getting the better of us, we all have the power to stop, breathe, and feel the loving counter energy that is there. Look into the eyes of someone you love. Gaze at the landscape; hear the birds. Feel the cells of your body feeding your life, giving you another day to enjoy. Watch the world around you, the smiles, hear the laughs. It is easier to recognize pain and suffering but that does not mean you must only focus on that. Ask the positive energy surrounding you for peace, love, joy, and a recognition of the miracles that surround you.

Exhale.

Find that space between thoughts and actions when breathing. Your body needs deep belly breathing to regulate your nervous system all day. There is a misconception that you should breathe deep only in moments of anxiety, depression or anger. The best practice is to breathe deep all day whenever you can. This will hinder your system from entering states of distress quickly. If you do fall into an unpleasant state, it will be much easier to release yourself from it. Breathing also allows you to practice mindfulness. Healthy minds rest in the present only. Honor yourself and practice conscious breathing.

Win.

Sometimes we do not see victory in our everyday lives, the tough parts shine though. Focus on the "wins" no matter how big or small. What are your victories? For every action there is an equal reaction. Remember this when you choose your patterns of thought. Allowing negativity to flow continually without noticing the equal positivity, which is there, will work against you. There is no excuse for ignoring your victories in life. Waking up, observing the beauty in life, seeing the sunshine, smelling the coffee brewing, hugging a pet, friend, family member, being able to go to work, having a roof over your head, food in your cupboards, driving a car, having basic freedoms; all of these things are victories in your life. Embrace each one. Take in moments as they come.

_____

_____

_____

Release.

The idea of mediation scares some people. They think it is something odd, or that they will do it wrong. In truth, focusing on the breath and breathing with intention is meditation. Anyone can do it and you will feel the difference practicing this. You will feel awake, prepared, and much calmer. Most people struggle with control. This results in some feeling anger, anxiety, depression, or fear. The way to let go? Breathing. Today, start the practice and see how you feel about yourself by the end of the day. You will continue this way of living once you make it a habit.

_____

_____

_____

Life is a gift.

Remember that life itself is a gift. Even in times of struggle, you have this life at your disposal to make some choices. How will you decide to live? In fear or joy? With hate or love? Honestly or with deception? Will you enjoy each moment or live in the past or future? You are the only one who can create your life. Nothing that happens to you and or nothing anyone does to you has any bearing on how you choose to receive the gift of life.

_____

_____

_____

Expansion.

Spread your wings; expand your world. There are no limits to what your soul can achieve. Envision riding a wave as the ups and downs flow in and out of your life. Expand the vision for your life. What path have you been on? Is there a better road for your growth and success? Magnify your horizon and explore all that is out there for you to discover.

_____

_____

_____

Review your life.

Take inventory of what you are spending your precious moments on.

What serves your soul? What grows you as a person? What can you let go? What do you have to keep and why? What would your life look like if you could choose every aspect at this moment? How can you align your daily actives with what your mind, body and spirit are asking of you? Sometimes, things cannot all change, but your perception can. How can you look at your life situation differently? How can you embrace the present each day? What can you accept from others? Where is your boundary? What is the means to an end?

_____

_____

_____

Protection.

Letting go and asking the positive energies of the universe for protection against fear will allow you space for happiness. If you feel eager or worried know that you can ask for peace and it will come from you deciding to focus today on love, living in the moment, and the power of goodness. Fear has no place in your life. When praying or asking for help, remember that will come in a form of an opportunity for you to take or possibly a decision for you to make. Situations will be put on your path to answer your queries. Remedies come from your decisions.

Nurture yourself.

Time for reflection and personal rebirth. As the days pass, we have memories, and we make new memories. We have responsibilities. We have a new view of the world with every year that goes by. Relive memories; rewrite the experiences that have hurt you. You have the right to explore your childhood. Work with the little you that lives deep inside. As an adult you can now make sense of what has happened over time. If you are a parent, nurture your children and observe how you are building the adult that your children will soon become. What do you want their inner child to know once their adult self covers him/her up? Nurturing is the ultimate form of healing the mind, body, and soul.

_____

_____

_____

Putting it all together

Your existence is a work in progress. Each day there is an opportunity to learn more about how you fit into the web of life. It is important to go easy on yourself and make a commitment that you will never stop learning about positive personal growth. Continue to explore what will help you to live to your highest potential.

Everyone has so much to offer during their brief time on this earth. Each moment is sacred. Every day counts and offers so much to people who open their eyes and hearts to it. Looking at the days as time given to you to cherish and embrace, even when you experience hardship, will make your efforts to grow and heal valuable.

You are important. You are enough. You have unlimited potential and abilities.

Peace and love to you always.

~ REFLECTIONS ~

CPSIA information can be obtained
at www.ICGtesting.com
Printed in the USA
BVHW072203060421
604336BV00005B/682

9 781982 255084